When A D.A.B.

Spills The Tea

"I always win"

– Bridget Hilliard

This book is dedicated to:

Any and everybody that has came and gone in my life. Whether it was for a reason or just a season.

Acknowledgments

My Son, D.Wash for motivating me to never give up. My daughter, Kivana who always remind I'm their Supa Woman. My Momma, Rockin Robbin always letting me know never let a nicca get the best of you. My Grandma, Messy Bessie for always keeping me on top of my game and raising me and my son having my back rather right or wrong. My annoying lil sister and brother (Tae & Lil Dwayne) who do anything I ask even if they don't want to. My cousin, Jon the Stylist who puts me on a pedestal so high only God can catch me but he always right there to never let me hit the ground. My friend Kai the Trashy Diva who is more like a sister who thinks she can tell me what to do knowing I'm gone do what I want do when I want do how I want to do it. My best friend Nikki the Nail Trapper who's thee ultimate best knowing that I'm gone do exactly what I want so she say how she feels and move right along. I can't leave out my friends Krazy Kay and Heavy who sat up with me for 2 days straight just to edit the book. Jaina for putting the finishing touches on the book before publishing. And last but not least my lil cousin ,Eboni who actually inspired me to write this book.

Table of Contents

Intro

I've been a Down Ass Bitch for a long time and now here I am sitting back, thirty two years old, thinking: *'Is this really just who I am? Is this all a part of my character?'*

I can remember back to my first boyfriend-- in middle school, seventh grade. I was sitting on the porch of my daddy's house on Mazant Street. A guy kept riding past on his bicycle. You could tell he was a street dude hustling because he was riding back and forth. Always looking like he was up to something. *'What is he doing?'* I remembered asking to myself.

He kept saying stuff off and on, throwin shots. I was 13 years old and interested, sitting there with a look that screamed *'Hey, boy.'* Soon enough, he was sitting on my daddy's porch, talking to me like we had been neighborhood friends. He gave me his number and we continued to talk afterwards until he eventually became my boyfriend. My initial impression of him as a hustler was on point because throughout middle school he was doing just that: *hustling*. He was selling drugs, buying me stuff and doing this that and the other. Then, he got locked up. During that time, I became pregnant. Yes, pregnant at 13 years old and I wasn't pregnant for him. Not only was I confused about how I was going to explain this to my family, but how was I going to tell my boyfriend I was pregnant but not for him. Remember, he's in jail at this time.

At this time I didn't know what jocing was all about, but he would try and get his brother, momma, *anybody* to call me on three-way. I was just a kid. I didn't really know what was going on. Of course, at the time, I thought it was kind of cute that he would go out of his way to get time o the phone with me and I guess that's where it all started with me really being a Down Ass Bitch!

Prologue

So, let's get into this whole being a Down Ass Bitch thing: After years and years of the same situations and falling for similar types of dudes that I thought were so hot, I noticed a pattern. You could even say that I had a type. Like, I got an adrenaline rush when I saw a street nicca. That specific feeling of hype when checking how he dressed, his demeanor, his character, his attitude, his *everything* was almost overwhelming. I looked for that one dude that stood out, that said, "Bitch, I'm the boss." It just did--and still does--something to me. Craving street niccas came with ups and downs. There was just something about the way they made me feel. It put me in a position where I was willing to ride or die for the nicca.

Whatever happened, I was going to be there.

By the time I hit high school, I met this dude. He was hype -- real hyped. Everybody knew him, except me. I remember going to my cousin's house and this hype ass nicca showed up. "'Who is this?" I asked. She told me he was her lil' brother. "I never knew you had a lil' brother." She told me that they had been in foster care together.

He was curious too. He wanted to know who I was. "Who is your fine ass cousin?" he had asked, confidently and just standing his ground. I was like, *'Boy, I got a boyfriend'*, but he was in jail and this nicca didn't care nothing about a boyfriend.

Low and behold, He was just what I was attracted and I had caught the attention of another street nicca. But he was hustling on a whole different level. My life felt like I had moved up on a step-ladder.

It started with a nicca doing a lil' something like buying shoes, this, that and the other. *'Now, I'm a little more mature, with a son and responsibilities. I needed more than that, I needed a boss nicca!"* Someone who's really making moves. He was doing that, we started going on dates and hanging out. It was fun at first, but then shit hit the fan and he had hoes coming from every angle. It was baby momma drama all over the place. At that point, I was turned up. I was with the shits. I was with the pull-ups, the jumping outta cars wanna fight you, bust your windows, type of shit. Before you know it I had to fight his baby momma and whoever was tripping. If that wasn't enough, this nicca would fight me too.

Oh baby! When things didn't go his way, or he felt like I was gonna leave, he wanted to fight and we would tear it down. After all the fights with him, his hoes, and even his family, I still stayed down with this nicca. However, when I started really getting out there and meeting other niccas it was soon over for him. I started to see the bigger picture. I remembered telling myself, *'This nicca ain't worth all the shit I'm going through.'* There were niccas with bigger money, bigger status and ultimately bigger problems. When I tell you that situation was crazy, I mean big time crazy. I'm not going to go into those details. I'll just move on to the next situationship.

I was like 17 years old, leaving the New Orleans Center-- a mall in the Central Business District known as the CBD. I remember it like it was yesterday. My friend Buffy and I were leaving the New Orleans Center to catch the (Galvez Bus) and a green

Tahoe or Yukon--I can't really remember--but someone was blowing their horn as they turned the block. A dude was trying to holla at us. Now back then when a nicca holler and you walking that's an opportunity for a ride (LOL). "Nicca, are you going to give us a ride or not?" we questioned.

"Of course," he said yeah, not thinking these niccas might kidnap us, we hopped right in the truck. His potna asked us, "How y'all know we not gone kidnap y'all?" Buffy and I both started laughing and said that we weren't going down without a fight. I got in the front with the driver and the passenger got in the back with Buffy. So, they started talking introducing themselves to us. The nicca in the front was an old nicca who thought he was young. My lil' fast ass was 17 with a two year old. He was sitting in that bitch like a big dog talking shit like, *'wassup, but you too young,'* while I was like, *'age ain't nothing but a number.'* I was definitely too young. We exchanged numbers and I think maybe after a month or so later, we finally talked again. Fast-forward 12 or so years later, we still talked. Crazy, right? That was one of the biggest situationships that I was the ultimate Down Ass Bitch.

Later on down the line I found out out that the nicca was married. The nicca sold big dope, too. He was a big boss nicca. He walked around the city like, *'yeah I'm that nicca'* and everybody knew who he was and everybody knew me by association. He was in love with that lil' girl, as the streets would say. That situationship involved some of the most funniest, craziest times in my life. Me hanging with him taught me how to hustle. I didn't care if it was selling drugs, pussy or scamming. Whatever it was, he gave me the game.

He also taught me that as a woman, I didn't even know my worth. He would always say, "You wonder why I never had sex with you until you made 18? You were a child and I wouldn't want anybody having sex with my child. I did that to show you even though I was attracted I had respect for you."

He bought me my first car when I graduated from high school. He made sure everything I needed was in order. He made sure I didn't want for *ANYTHING*. It gave me a form of security. He gave me the mindset that if I was loyal, I would be rewarded. Did your parents reward you when you were good and punish you when you weren't? That's what it was like for the first two years with this nicca, because as long as I was going to school and doing what I was supposed to do, there was nothing that I wanted for.

He bought my first Gucci bag and he was the first man besides my dad and grandfather to buy me diamonds.

Expensive gifts were normal. He would have the boosters pulling up to my grandma's house, popping the trunk and getting out whatever I wanted or needed. As I started getting older and getting in my groove, I wanted to get my own money. I wanted to be put in the game. He agreed in a way. He told me, *'All you have to do is be here, and do what I need you to do.'* Now that I look back, it was a form of manipulation. Yes, I know it was a lot after 12 years of being in a "situationship". I do know one thing: the nicca really loved me and he jeopardized everything fucking with me. And I did the same thing: hitting the road and making trips, picking up this and picking up that, but it always came with a gift. As long as I was being loyal, I was getting rewarded, so at that time it worked for me. While sitting around and getting into everything that he was into, I picked up on everything. I'd sit there and act like I didn't know what's going on, but the whole time I was learning. I was watching everything. And by everything I mean everything: whatever it was, from the drugs, to the fake checks, to credit cards scams. Even down to manipulating my way to get whatever I wanted. The mind frame of being the boss, the same energy I got from seeing what he did, made me feel like I could do it too. I took everything in. I took it all and I ran with it. I started living my life being a Down Ass Bitch.

CHAPTER 1 - What is a DAB?

DAB is an acronym for "Down Ass Bitch"

A DAB is a chick who is loyal for whatever the cause she feels is beneficial to her.

Life in the city after Hurricane Katrina was so lit and with both the good and bad. It had to be summer 2006 and New Orleans was back poppin'. It was really a party palace. Every club was poppin', from *Keywest* to *Rockafella* to *Club Escape.* Like, literally everywhere, it was lit. I don't know what it was, but after the storm, when everyone started coming back home, the city was just going crazy with fun and we were living our best lives way before the term "Best Life" was heard of.

Me and my girls were running the streets every day heavy, heavy. All the big time niccas that were anybody knew us and even the ones who weren't as popular knew us as well. They knew we were with the shits. We had all the hottest niccas in almost every hood. All of us had someone from each crew.

Saturday night was the best night by far. *Rockfella 2.5* was club of choice on a Saturday. Being the fun girl who was very outspoken and known all around New Orleans, I stayed turned up, I love to dance and have a good time. The dating scene for me was very slim pickings, because I like what I like even though I had plenty of offers and was always being asked to go to dinner (or just do something for a nicca to be in my company), I always had a particular type and if you didn't fit that criteria, I wasn't really paying you any attention. One night, my lil' cousin and I were in *Rockafella 2.5.* She was vibing with this dude who had been flirting with her, I was standing there trying to figure out who he was with. I was looking at dude, why he never came over with his potna. I was locked in because I felt like I knew him from somewhere. As a matter of fact, I was certain I knew him. But wait this nicca was so hot. I really can't even begin to put it into words. His demeanor was very aggressive and said, *'Bitch I'm the man.'* Now that I know him, I know that at that time that was really how he felt. He was standing directly in front the bar with Rock and Revival jeans on, a Von Dutch snapback that was pulled real low, but his face was still noticeable. He had hazel eyes and a scar on his face that anyone who ever saw him would remember. He was definitely very laid back, peeping the scene like, *'I'm here but I don't wanna be bothered so don't come fuck with me.'* Now his mans was always on a totally different kick. He stayed in a bitch's face and was just really more outgoing. That's just who he was.

I was trying my best to peep ole boy out and find out who he really was. I had seen him a few times before in this spot, but it wasn't on a consistent basis. That told me that *(A)* he probably had an ole lady, or *(B)* he was really on his boss shit and not playing the club scene like that. Every now and then, he only came out to see what was going on. *I was sitting back giving him the eye like, 'Wassup with you?' and he was looking at me as if to say, 'I see you, what's up?'*

But I was still looking at him like, *'Yeah, nicca I'm feeling you and I'm trying to see what's up.'* I really thought I was going with my move because I had enough of the eye fucking so I told his potna to tell his man to here. He already knew that I was feeling him and he came over and introduce himself, yada yada yada. So, we started talking and we exchanged numbers. Turns out, he really did have an ole lady, but I made it clear that his situation was the least of my concerns. We really started hitting it off, going on dates here and there. Chilling at my spot, smoking, etc. We always had so much fun together. Smoking and fucking became our favorite things to do. For a couple of months, that was the vibe and I really started digging him because the energy I felt when I saw him in the club was on point with who he really was. He wasn't loud or flamboyant and he was very selective in how he move.

As a matter of fact, I had never heard his name ring in the streets messing with anyone. That made me even I never really was always hard for me to take dudes serious that messed with buku hoes. I'm very selfish, so once a nicca tells me he fucking with me, I expect to be the top priority and I really don't care who else gets their time or anything else. Yeah, I'll respect it if a nicca tells me he got an ole lady but that comes with some guidelines, I was just that type of bitch.

I knew that he was in a situationship with someone before me. I chose to "Get Down" with what he had going on because I wanted to fuck with him and all the other shit really was irrelevant to me, especially the ole lady. I played my part though, it was a few times I would want to holler at him, but knowing his situation I kept my guards up and stayed out the way. He didn't need to say all the disclaimer stuff because I knew what it was from the start.

As much as I was feeling him, he was feeling me too. As soon as he would get outside, he would call me and we would hang out. He always kept his word. And that's one thing I respected about him. Respect goes a long way. Your word is everything. He was fucking with me tough and I started feeling some type of way. I put all my other niccas on the back burner and I was really fucking with him the long way usually, if I play it like that, I need you to show me that you're on the same type of time, and pay to play. He wasn't really doing all that. Yeah, he would take me places and spend while we were together, but he wasn't popping it off like I was accustomed to. So, I got in my bag and started falling back. I felt like I was getting the short end of the stick and that didn't sit well with me. One day I asked him for $200 just to see if I was right and he told me he didn't have it. I was puzzled as to why he said that, because I knew he had it. Everything about him let me know he had the money. I really felt played because we were fucking around tough and vibing, but he never offered to pay a bill or for miscellaneous stuff. In hindsight, I knew he didn't offer, because I didn't put that on the table.

Knowing what I know now, before I go into any situationship, I lay my expectations out before I get in too deep because a nicca will only live up to what you let him know you expect. I really didn't have the grounds to be upset because I never put it on the table for him. So when I did ask and he shut it down, I shut him down and never talked to him again. I didn't know that five years later, we'd reconnect and I'd be his Down Ass Bitch for the next eight years.

CHAPTER 2 - Trust

On September 17, 2007, my dad was killed in a motorcycle accident. I was going through it. I'm definitely a daddy's girl. In his eyes, I was his prized possession. He treated me as if nothing else mattered and with him gone, any man that tried to come in my life, I looked for the same feeling. Sometime in November, I met this nicca that kind of looked like Beanie Seagal, real hood and rough, but to me he was the sweetest. At that time, I was really vulnerable because the death of my father was still fresh. This dude had just came home from prison after doing 9 years and he loved the ground I walked on. I was happy too genuinely. I felt that it was what I needed, but it wasn't what I wanted.

The money was my main priority. That was my main focus. Once I started healing from the death of my dad was when I started fucking up the relationship. I knew that if I needed anything or wanted to get that bag up quicker, I could always go back to that old nicca with the dope money. My loyalty had already been established and as long as I was on his team, it really didn't matter because the money was going to constantly flow. Don't get me wrong, I loved the times all that good stuff that came with my current dude, but at that time my motive was the money and that dope boy money was what I wanted. He couldn't give me time and comfort, he thought he could make it up with other things in the form of gifts or money. However, at the time I was young and naïve, so I allowed him to substitute gifts and money for time. Accepting that cost me a great relationship with someone I knew loved me dearly and did everything he could to make me happy. I fucked it all up.

Fast forward, I found myself in a committed relationship with the same nicca that didn't give me $200. It was some time in 2011 when I received a call from my brother's ex-girlfriend and she told me that someone was looking for me. Mind you, we are a couple of years apart in age, so I wasn't thinking we knew many of the same people, especially not someone close enough to relay a message to me. Of course, my Curious George head ass was tickled pink, so I was anxious to know who was trying to get in contact with me. When she told me TJB, I was like, *'What? The dude with the pretty eyes and the scar on his face?'* Yep, that was him. No lie, I was all excited, but in my mind, I was like, *'You the same nicca that didn't give me $200 dollars.'*

I knew this nicca had better been trying to give me that $200 or he might as well exit left. So, I asked where he was and she said jail. *JAIL*...................What did that nicca want with me when he was locked up? But I told her to give him my number.

The next day he called and I answered, sounding all hood in my New Orleans voice. Of course, he matched my excitement with his *'Wassam'*. I played as if I didn't know who it was and asked, "Who is this?" He answered, *'man don't play with me'*, and of course his attitude and disposition was the same as it was when we first met and to be honest, that attitude always kept me interested. He really had always been cocky and his attitude was so bossed like, *'Bitch, I'm the man and I know I'm the man.'*

So we get to running it and talking about the things that were going on in my life and really catching up. He was giving me advice on taking things slower and just embracing the moments. I confided in him about my previous relationship and how it was so fresh that I was still caught up in the fact that I wasn't ready and that's why it didn't work out. I just wasn't what he needed in the relationship. I wasn't able to give, so it dissolved. We talked about me just moving around the city and going to school and doing hair. From that day, and everyday to follow, him and I talked. From being so in tune with each other and me being able to understand with his situation, we started building trust between us. We would talk about everything. A year later, I went to visit him for the first time. I was so nervous that, on the way there, I stopped like five times to shit because my nerves were so bad. The visit was amazing. We clicked, but I was still nervous. We continued to talk on the phone and ended up getting emotionally attached to each other. During one of our many conversations, I found out that he was eligible for parole the next year. I was super geeked because I started making plans with him being a part of my life. Pretty soon, I was going to see him every week. Of course, I was still doing my own thing but, at that moment, it seemed like we both needed each other for emotional stability. I wasn't his ole lady or even speaking to him when he got locked up. It wasn't any beef but looked how things turned around. We talked about the reason for him wanting to get at me because I thought he was looking for someone to joce but, of course, he let it be known that I wasn't the only one he was talking to. I told him how I felt about those $200 and I let him know that he was going to pay dearly for not giving it to me. Of course, every time I got the chance to get something out of him, I did.

Yes, even while he was in jail. For three years straight, he sent me Green Dots to make sure I was straight. I was going harder with going to see him and sending pictures and answering his calls and, on some real shit, that built trust and loyalty with both of us. I played my position and I 'Got Down' with what he was going through. So much that we were all in and on a different level than when we had started because my loyalty and trust had been proven by my actions.

It was December 2012 and we were all the way in. This nicca had asked me to marry him. He was coming home the following year so I was all for it. The way he made me feel seemed like it gave me an adrenaline rush, but in a good way and I loved every second of it. I was working, in school, and hustling. I wasn't even sexually active any more this nicca had me gone from the jail house. I had changed up the things I used to do because I was ready for this new chapter with him. I wasn't thinking about being with anyone or even having sex with anyone, which was another reason why we worked so well because he could only provide the emotional side. I was shocked over the effect he had on me and we weren't even having sex. By this time, I had met his entire family and, of course, they loved me. His mom would always call me and was sure to let me know that he was serious about marrying me. Although he was ready to get married, I wasn't going to go that far due to the circumstances. To symbolize our engagement, we decided to get matching tattoos on our ring fingers. I couldn't wait to visit to see his and show him mine. I went to visit him the following Sunday and just couldn't stop smiling we laughed and talked the whole visit. His mother's reaction to our relationship made me feel even better. Every

Christmas Eve, I give a huge party. His entire family came over that year. It all was so real; nothing was hidden, nothing was out of place. The only thing missing was him physically being there. At that time, I felt it was the perfect thing, only to find out he wasn't coming home for the next seven years.

Chapter 3- Loyalty

A few weeks went by and I still hadn't told anybody, not even my best friend, Red. I was still going to work and school, pretending like everything was alright. I put on a face to make it seem as if nothing was out of the ordinary. Every time the phone rung and it was him, I felt empty. I pretty much stopped going to visit and got to a place where it was game time. I felt finessed. Like, in my mind, all I could think was that it was time for me to finesse a little too. When I say I didn't give a fuck who it was or how it happened, I mean it. I had to get back in my groove. I wasn't about to be anybody's wife. So, it was game time, time to be who I wanted to be and do what I know worked for me: Get Down and be a Down Ass Bitch.

I have always had that gift for gab. I've always been very flirtatious and in the midst of things. As far as my personality goes, it always put me in a position where I was *that* girl. It was really nothing for me to go back to partying and having a good time physically, but mentally and emotionally, I was stuck. My state of mind, the way I thought, changed drastically. My goals were different. My *focus* was different. My goal wasn't to walk down the aisle and look this nicca--who I'd been jocing for the past three years--in the face and be his wife. It just wasn't there any more.

something that I wanted so bad, I'd be ok. Having niccas do almost anything for me and drool over me when I walked in a room, was the best. The spotlight was on me! I felt like Mitch when he walked in the club on "Paid in Full." I always loved that person from a little girl. I was always in the limelight as a little girl--dancing school, ballet, whatever. So I said I was going to tap into that side of me. I was going to give it my all. I gave something that I wanted for my future and I got let down, so I thought that I might as well do something that I always wanted to do. To be a star, given a chance, was what I really wanted.

I decided I was going to say fuck being a wife, fuck the marriage. Fuck that life. I was going to move to Atlanta, do hair during the day, dance at night, and find one of them rich niccas to sponsor it all at the end. It's funny, but it was true how you could say what you want. I didn't really give a fuck, but it was either that or be a wife. There wasn't really an in between either: you're either in wifey mode or you in heaux mode, whatever you want to call it. You have to be about your money, either way. You can't be playing around, doing shit, and having nothing to show for it. Everybody has to have a motive or goal. In life, you need to have a target. I had a new target and I was not getting finessed in the process. I was doing all the finessing. I hadn't even left New Orleans yet, of course, and any nicca that came my way knew I wasn't playing. When I tell you if it was not about that bag there wasn't anything we could talk about. At that time, it was still lil' shit like, I need to do something at the shop, I need $1200, I need $500--lil' shit that wasn't dates. We weren't doing any of that. That's just how I was living.

I was living in a bitter, torn place. I didn't care whose feelings I hurt, whose neck I stepped on because this nicca had already stepped on my heart. I still had this lil' spot in the back of my mind that said before I did anything, I needed to think about the fact he wanted me to be his wife. I knew with the way that I was moving, I had to leave the city. I couldn't live in New Orleans.

There was just too much I had to face. I couldn't be here and still be labeled as TJB's girl. I couldn't do that. I was so broken. Of course, eventually, I had to tell my family and my friends, the people who were looking forward to him coming home as much as I did, that he wasn't. In the midst of this, we were talking every now and again, but it was nothing like it used to be.

Every single time he called, I was handling him--just on some shit like, *'You know I'm really not feeling you.'* I felt as if he was still trying to finesse me to believe that the only reason he wasn't home was because he got caught with a phone and they took his good time. For the life of me, I didn't believe that and I didn't really care what was said or what was done. He could have gotten the judge to tell me that and I still wouldn't have believed it. Because at that point, I didn't even give a fuck. I felt such a deep sense of betrayal that I knew there was no turning back from this. With me being so loyal, I still ended up picking up the phone, still sent pictures; I still put a few dollars on his books, whatever. I still had the thought of, *'I'm not fucking with you like that, bruh.'* The trust we had and respect I had for him had been cut in half. I trusted and believed that he loved me. I know he loves me; I knew that, but I also knew he was *selfish*. Sometimes, you're in a position to where you should be selfish, however when somebody comes into your life and has been loyal to you to this extent, it should mean something. So, mentally, he put me in a position to where I didn't care about anything. Like I said before, I was living off of hurt and that gassed me, gave me fuel to just do whatever I wanted to do. I got back into the game: swiping, scamming, dancing. It was just like, *'Fuck It. I'm about to get this bag, and if a nicca wasn't talking about no money, I aint wanna talk period'* I still, for some reason, had this man and what we built in the forefront of my mind, because no matter what I did, no matter how much somebody showed me they liked me or wanted to be with me, I would never break.

I felt like I wasn't about to let another nicca break me down and have me fall in love again. If I were to be with anybody, I'd be with him when he came home.

That was how I felt. I broke a few hearts along the way but, you know, Lord forgive me for my sins. It wasn't like I said, *'I'm just going to break a heart, today.'* No! It wasn't like that at all. I didn't care just because someone was in their feelings. I wasn't about to get in my feelings and I really, pretty much, said that up front to any and everybody. Meanwhile during all this, I was still in love, that shit just don't go away. Whatever made me happy, or whatever I thought made me happy, at that moment was my priority, no longer me and him.

CHAPTER 4 - Stay Down, Come Up

I had my mind made up. I was moving to Atlanta. I said I'd do hair during the day and dance at night. I'd work my way through these city streets, meet a few niccas with a bag to get my money up until TJB comes home. I still wanted to be this nigga's wife because I knew he loved me for me. Even the stuff he didn't like. I just knew that nothing could make me *not* believe that. You know when a person wants to be with you and when a person just wants a fuck thang or if it's just about a coin. I was so sure because his mom and I were talking one day and she said, "I done seen my son with a lot of woman and I know my son, but I don't know what you did to him. I never seen him like this."

From that moment on, it gave me a sense of

security. She wasn't one of those old raunchy hood moms that would sell you a dream, going on and on about *'My son this and my son that.'* She was not like that at all. That stuck with me, no matter what I did. It never was out in the open. It never was blasted or boasted about. I continued to live and fight through my pain. I was dancing, modeling, and doing hair staying busy it gave me something I was missing. It gave me the energy he took from me. The limelight made me feel like, *'nicca I'm Supa D, I'm still D'wayna. I'm still BAD.'* I never wanted anybody to see how hurt I really was. I wanted everyone to think I was just as happy as I was when I thought this nicca was getting out of jail.

I never told the world that the engagement was off and he wasn't coming home. I just lived through it. I let it die down.

A few months went by and my birthday was coming up. I had bought this new *BMW X5*. I woke up one day, thinking, *'I'm moving to Atlanta. I'm going with my move.'* I had to do what I felt was best for me. I had to get that money for a better situation for me and my son. I knew that if I was really going, I had to go with a plan. I had already had a mindset that *'I always win'*. I asked my son, who was 14 years old at the time, "Are you gone come to Atlanta with me or stay in New Orleans?" He said he wanted to stay and I was fine with that. About three weeks later, I packed up my truck and shot out.

At that time, I was really up. I really had a situation going on where the money didn't stop. It was coming in like clockwork. I had this guy giving me $5000 here, $2500 there, $1200 there, $5000 here, you name it. I was thinking, *'Shit, if I'm doing numbers like that in New Orleans, I already know what I could do in the A. I gotta go.'* I was comfortable with the plan of doing hair during the day and dancing at night, but it never really happened. I danced at night, but never managed to do hair during the day (lmao).

One day, I went to this casting call for a reality tv show. After the casting call, I was one of the top 3 picks. I met these girls Tia and Lela the vixen. We hit it off on the first day and started going out and fucking the city up. We were like the stars of the show. A few of the other girls were pretty cool, but they didn't really like us because all three of us had that same type of energy: we arrived and we were the stars. The three of us weren't mean, nasty, or shady to anyone else, but our energy together made people feel some kind of way.

Lela was like a lil' sister, while Tia and I were like two peas in a pod. We'd fuss, damn near about to kill each other, but we had the same goals at the end of the day: *get to the bag.* We were going out in the Atlanta partying damn near every night, and you know, of course, she knew about the whole TBJ situation. She was like, *'Well, what you gone do?'* I told her that whatever happened when he come home happened. I told her that I was focusing on Supa D because TBJ wouldn't be out for a few more years.

At that time, Tia was working on her hair line, while I was working on a lipstick line. I got someone to invest in the whole lipstick brand, bought a couple thousand dollars worth of lipstick and it sold out. I reup'd a few times, but I was still on some bullshit. My mind was still somewhere else. I was getting the money, but I wasn't keeping the money. All I was doing was partying and spending. The money was just going, going, and going. It hit me sometime in 2015. The show wasn't really doing well and we hadn't gotten picked up by a network. I was still partying and the lipstick brand wasn't really doing anything for me. Everything had sold out and I didn't have anything to show for it--except memories and bags, shoes, and clothes. All bullshit. I was puzzled. What was I going to do?

By this time, TJB and I were kind of back to talking more frequently, but I was still playing that role. I wasn't going back to the point I was at before with him. I couldn't see myself ever being that vulnerable. He was still locked up and I was still waiting for him to come to me. I was getting it out the mud, risking my life and freedom, doing all kind of shit to keep the money flowing. At that point, you couldn't tell me anything. I was in Atlanta, seeing all these young 28-30 year old millionaires doing something with their lives and thinking, *'Why ain't I no millionaire?'*

I was just looking at all the shit around me for motivation, but I was still fucking putting my all into the fast life. That went on for about another year, until I started feeling like something was going to slow me down.

I had an appearance in Tampa, Florida in 2016. My two best friends from back home, Diva and Red, came with me. We got to Florida and had a great time, prior to me putting my trap bag in the car. I had some shit I had to do, but I never thought to take the bag out. The event was pretty cool and I never cared about how much I made with my events because, for me, it was just something to do. I had a buzz going: my Instagram numbers were jumping and I was getting more bookings people started to really know who I was. I had hosted a few parties and was making more money. I didn't really care what people thought or had to say. I just wanted to feel like I was doing something besides trying to be the wife of a nicca in jail.

CHAPTER 5 - Been Down

The next day, or two we were leaving Florida. Diva and I dropped Red off at the airport, but me and Diva got into it for whatever reason. This bitch didn't want to drive, completely disregarding the fact that I was the one who drove all the way there. She refused to drive, so I was pissed and wanted that bitch out my fucking car and out my face. I pulled over to smoke a blunt and mash out. Pulling off, I was apparently flying down the highway. I think the officer said I was doing 96 in a 65 on *I-75*. He said when I flew past him, I shook his fucking car. I saw the bitch fly off that median to come after me. There wasn't any weed in the car, so I wasn't tripping.

I just didn't want to get pulled over. I was thinking Diva was on papers and she wasn't supposed to be out of the city. I didn't even think about the trap bag in the back of the car, but I was still thinking, *'Should I run this nicca and jump off the interstate and hide cause I ain't really got time for these fucking people.'*

I pulled over and as soon as he got to the window, he said, "You were going pretty fast. Were you smoking?"

I said, "Why would I be smoking and driving, speeding at that? I'm gonna be honest with you, I smoked before I left where I was, but I wasn't smoking and driving."

So, he ran my name and came back and asked me to step out the car. He asked me all kind of questions. It wasn't anything I never heard before. He then asked to search the car. I didn't care because there wasn't any

They let her go, but keep in mind that we were three hours from Atlanta in some ole country ass town where they were tweaking for a conviction. There wasn't shit going on out there and they were taking my black ass to jail. I was pissed off and all I could think about was that if this nicca wasn't in jail, I wouldn't even be doing any of this. Some may say I was wrong for feeling like that, but that's how I felt. I wasn't exactly blaming him because shit, it is what it is, and I was gonna do me, but I knew if he was home he wasn't having it.

The next morning Red bonded me out and got the rental out the pound. Diva had got in touch with Tia in Atlanta to come and pick her up. Diva then flew to New Orleans before he probation officer found out she was out of town. I shot straight to Atlanta. We knew something was going to happen, but when? A couple of months later, Diva called to give me some news. They had jammed her up on some other shit and her probation officer decided to put it all together. Now, I was fucked for real. My right hand was fucked up and I have an open charge now. What the fuck was going on in my life? Like, what was going on? I tried to figure out what I was going to do now that Diva was in jail. I didn't trust anybody else and I knew for a fact Red wasn't having it. She wasn't going to jail for fucking around with anything--she had a job and she thought I needed to get one too. A job, like a real job. I had built up this image and this persona, but where the fuck was I going to work if I tried? I was back to my old ways of finessing at its finest. I was going from Miami, to L.A, to Vegas. One day, I was on my way to the airport to go to Vegas and got pulled over once again.

The car smelled like weed. These people tore that truck upside down looking for it. I told the police, "You wasting your time if you think I'm that stupid to smoke weed and have pounds of weed in the car." This man ran my name and turns out, I had a fugitive warrant since 2014. It was 2016, and they were telling me about a warrant in 2014. I was confused. I ended up in jail and I remember thinking, *'Lord if I get out of this, I promise I'll get it together.'* I got out about eight days later. Those eight days took me to a whole other mind frame because of the women I met and ministered to. Like, ok if you want to finesse, finesse, but that other shit will get your ass in a world of trouble. I was going to be locked up for real, I couldn't see my best friend or the nicca I was supposed to be marring. I remember thinking to myself, *'It's only you out here. You got to hold it down, you have to be that Down Ass Bitch. You gotta be in another realm. You have to get that bag.'*

I went back to Atlanta after they transferred me to Louisiana. I got out of jail, got back to Atlanta and still, mentally, was lost, but I knew I couldn't go back to jail. That was all I knew: that I couldn't go back to jail. I didn't give a shit. I just knew jail wasn't an option. So, I said I was going to do what I do best: finesse. Every chance I got, I was finessing. I wouldn't have cared if I had to go to a nigga's house and clean up, cook for him and look cute. I was doing whatever I had to do to get that bag and not do anything illegal. I didn't want to dance anymore because I felt like that tie had come and gone. But nobody ever saw me at a strip club. They couldn't say that or put that on me. That was assumed. That was something I did in secret time. Now I wasn't feeling it anymore. I wanted a family, the family I planned with TJB. What was going on? I was in the limelight. People knew me, but I still wasn't happy. Something was still missing. Every time I looked around it was something else, but still, when he called, everything seemed like it was going to be alright. I believed that, but when the call ended, that emptiness was still there.

CHAPTER 6 - Down For Him

I heard that same emptiness I felt in his voice the day he called, crying like a baby, to tell me that his mother passed away. At that moment, nothing else mattered. All I knew was that I had to stay down with him until the very end. The relationship his mother and I built was crazy. Like, she never treated me like a daughter-in-law, she treated me like one of her own. It was weird because I don't do in-laws. His family and my very first boyfriend, the nicca that was supposed to be my husband, were the only families that were genuine and loyal. We're still close to this day. I could only imagine such a great loss. All she longed for was the day he got out of jail. That was all she wanted and she told me out of her own mouth, "I done seen him with all kind of women. I've seen TJB do all kind of things. I don't know what you did to my son, but I know for a fact he loves you." The relationship he and his mother had was beautiful. What they had always stuck with me and gave me a sense of security. It let me know that what we had was real. At this point, no matter what, I could not walk away. I left that same day and went to New Orleans. When that call ended, I threw my things in a bag and left. I talked to him back to back to back the whole ride from Atlanta to New Orleans. I'll never forget that day, that moment or anything about it. My next goal was to get to that jail and find a way for him to make it to the funeral because I knew with everything in me that if this man didn't get to the funeral, both of our lives would never be the same. He would have had to carry an open wound that would've never healed.

I made it to New Orleans after a six hour drive, then I drove four hours from New Orleans to the prison. His sister had already called the day that it happened and told the Warden, so they knew what to expect when I got there. I went to visit and I just couldn't stop looking at him, couldn't stop telling him that I love him, that I was sorry. I let him know that I was going to stay down, that I wasn't going anywhere. Visitations were only about an hour or two, it felt like five minutes this time. I had to go across the street, maybe around the corner, to the sheriff's office after visit, where the warden was located.

Visitations were only about an hour or two, it felt like five minutes this time. I had to go across the street, maybe around the corner, to the sheriff's office after visit, where the warden was located.

I spoke with a young girl at the front. I had already called to let them know I would be coming and the clerk at the window told me to wait for the warden's assistant. She said the warden would be back in thirty minutes. Two hours passed and there was no warden in sight, but I was patient. Over the last few years, I had been really working and praying on my patience and this was a test of that. As TJB called and called, I never got aggravated. I was putting him in good spirits. His voice was so full of concern, worried that he wouldn't be able to go to the funeral. I said, "Bae, I don't care what I gotta do, who I gotta pay, how long I have to stay." I promised him he would be at his mom's funeral. I walked back into the office and asked to speak with the lady. She told me that she had been calling and hadn't gotten a response. After the lady tried texting him, she finally got a reply. The warden had said to give him a call in a few minutes.

By this time, I was dying of starvation. I let her know that I was going to run to the store and be back. I went to Pizza Hut. TJB and I were still talking on the phone back and forth. "You still there?" he asked.

I said, "Bae, I'm not gone leave until it's handled." "You sure, you alright?"

"Listen, I been praying and God already told me it's done.

You just calm down, don't get upset and don't worry about nothing," I said. He said alright and I continued to pray. I don't think anyone would understand how much I prayed. I went back into the office and the warden's assistant asked me to come into her office.

I went in and she said the warden had been asking her different things. I looked at her and I said, "Listen, this man been in jail for nine years. His momma ain't ever miss a visit and, besides me, that's his backbone. If y'all don't want this jail flipped upside down, he has to be at this funeral."

I knew if that didn't happen it was going to be hell to tell the captain. I didn't care how much I had to pay. I asked her what I needed to do to make this happen. I explained how I knew that other inmates lost their mothers, but this particular situation was way different. The lady looked at me and said that she was going to do what she could. With the look she gave me, God had me sitting there being patient for a reason. She called the warden as she stepped out. After talking, they asked me what would I be willing to pay. I said, "I never did this before, so you tell me how it goes." She began to explain the different schedules of the officers and how they worked. She explained how the travel was so far, that it may cross over into another shift--basically, just telling me all the different things that could interfere with the transport. So, I asked her if she could find an officer willing to do it and I would pay whatever. She asked if I had the obituary or anything like that. I told her that I could get my sister-in-law to send it their way as soon as possible and we could go from there. If I'm not mistaken, I think the funeral was on Tuesday. I gave her my name, my address, my phone number and everything I could give her to show her that it was not a joke. I knew the lack of confirmation would have discouraged him, so when he called back, I told him everything was going to be alright. I told him we were probably going to have to pay for them to get an escort. All I could do was think, *'God come through.'*

I drove back to New Orleans to tell his sister everything that was going on. Soon as I arrived his sister asked, what happened. After telling her, she said, "Lord, I pray all is well. What is he going to do without you?"

"What am I gone do without him, if these people don't let him go to the funeral?" I asked.

We both knew that there was no guarantee from the jail in place, but I knew God wasn't going to put anything on us that we couldn't bare. I knew how much Momma Cherri, his sister, and I prayed and believed. I just knew God wouldn't let us down. So, I did have the confidence that everything would all work out in the midst of all the uncertainty. His sister kept saying, "Girl, a few hearts gone be broken." "What?"

"You know them girls gone be running to momma's funeral just so they can see him."

"I'm not worried about none of them. I don't have time for that and now is not the time for that," I said. She was just keeping it real. They were going to come and see whatever they could see. Instead of coming to pay respect to his momma, they were just trying see him. Most of these women hadn't seen him in nine or so years. If they did see him, they hit and miss because, for the last five years, I hadn't missed too many visits. I kept wondering why they wanted their feelings hurt, but it wasn't the time for any of that, so I just let it be. Monday came and I called, of course. They left me on hold for a time or two. I'd hang up and call back until, finally, I was able to speak with the lady from before. I went in and she said, "Well, we got the email that you sent and the warden approved it, nothing but God could have made this happen." "Trust me, with the God I serve, I knew it was gone happen,"

I said. "It probably won't be a long stay, but he will be at the service." I thanked her and asked if I needed to pay anything. She told me no and explained how an officer took the shift. I thanked her again and again. A feeling of relief washed over me. I released a deep sigh. I could only imagine the type of future he would have without ever seeing his mother for the last time. The craziest thing ever was that I had witnessed a similar situation with my daddy, but it was 10 times worse. His mother was killed by her other son while my daddy was in jail. My daddy was so strong, so much of a real nicca, that he looked in my face and told me, *'My momma raised me to be my brother's keeper.'* My daddy forgave his brother and walked in that church, to his momma's funeral, in shackles and never looked back. I remember it so vividly even though I was at such a young age. I knew that it was closure for him. I knew what I had to do. God prepares you for things even if you don't know when it will come full circle.

It was the day of the service and I had everything set up as I knew TJB would have. From the sprinter for the family, to the corsage, to the pendants, every detail I could think of was set to his standards. Even the flower arrangements were done as if he had ordered them himself. I was standing outside when I saw the sheriff car literally two blocks away and my heart melted. I was happy that he was able to be there, but I was sad that he had to endure this pain and that his whole family had to see him in shackles. The officer was amazing. He asked if I was his fiancé and I said that I was.

"I'm sorry for y'alls loss. I'm not going to let

him go in with handcuffs, but I can't take the shackles off," he said. He told me that he would sit in the back. His spirit was so amazing that it added to my feeling of relief. Any officer could have ended up bringing him to the funeral, but God had sent this particular one. We walked in and sat down and it was like... so unexplainable to go through something like that with someone you love, but I can honestly say, it definitely made it a tad bit easier for him to get through the service.

Of course we sat right in the front. There was something about this one particular troll that had me looking over at him and saying, "Oh, you mess with her, now?"

He said, "Right now, bruh?"I said, "Momma know me very well. We gone talk later." And I left it at that.

The service was beautiful. They spoke very well about her and everything was nice. We left out to greet the family and everybody was so ecstatic. The family was full of joy to see him. Older family members were in disbelief because they hadn't seen him in years. His older uncles told him not to lose me, especially since I was still with his ass despite him being in jail. They were all so funny, but this troll kept popping up. So then, I started thinking, *'What's the tea? Who is this?'* I wasn't paying that close of attention, but she was constantly in my peripherals. We left the church to go to the burial site and I saw the same troll walking out. *'Oh yeah, okay. So you feel like you somebody, sis? This nicca got you out of your body.*

It was not the time for that. I was there for my mother-in- law, not for anything else. I wasn't worried about him either. I was trying to make sure everything was in order to make the best of it. As we were leaving the grave site, sis thought she was going to make her move: she tried to hug on homeboy. Baby, she thought she was in but, before you know it, I had slapped homegirl's hand down. Condolences were over. She should have done that at the service.

The officer said, "You done got yourself in some trouble huh, boy?"

I really don't play like that. There I was, in the process of being down for my nicca, and you had a lil' cheerleader showing up at your mom's funeral like it was a regular visitation at the jail. We weren't about to do that. He told her, "go 'head you know what's up." I replied, "if she don't both of y'all gonna find out." We got to the repast and he looked at me and said, "you're crazy." I replied by asking, "Who was your boo at the service?"

"You serious?" he asked. I told him not to play with me and we laughed it off. I wasn't too bothered about it, but I still had 21 questions: like, what was really going on? The officer actually let him stay till about 3:00 p.m. It was so nice and everyone said their goodbyes. For us, from that day forward, things went back to normal. Well I thought it did.

CHAPTER 7 - Shut It Down

About a week went by, and I got a DM--
a strange DM. The DM was from someone
with an entire story detailing who they were
and why they felt the need to reach out to
me. This person acted as if they were telling
me their ex-friend was messing with TJB. It
had come from the troll. Baby, the troll wore
me thin. She sent screenshot after
screenshot of every single message from the
last month between her and him. I was
fuming pissed, I've never been the type to let
a bitch see me sweat. I wrote her back and
replied with a simple, *'Ok.'* The messages
were of him coming home to her, filled with
'I love you's and *'do you miss me*'s?
I was like, *'So, this is why she was so adamant
about being seen at the funeral.'* This was
why this troll was so pressed. He had a troll

thinking that he was going to be with her when he got home. I also figured out that the troll had been sending him money and visiting him. Oh, he was finessing. My stomach was balled up in 15 knots. All I could think about was that I had *just* told this bitch that I was going to stay down-- when I tell y'all I was hot!! This nicca was really playing jailhouse games, not even an hour after he called.

I'm a detective, on the low, when it comes to my nicca. I was comparing the times that they were texting to the times he was texting me. I was counting it all. You didn't text me, but at 8:05 there was something? I went that deep. When I answered the phone the next time he called, I couldn't cut corners. I didn't have time for it. We had a whole family crisis and he was doing this bullshit. That's why sis felt like she could do more than she should and that goes to show you that it's not what you do, it's how you do it. Niccas will do whatever they need to do for them to win, period! He had a fiancé willing to marry him, he had the nerve to have side hoes thinking *they* were the main bitch--I went nuts. I said, "You got something you want to tell me?" I started reading everything she sent me. After the third or fourth sentence, I could hear him screaming into the phone, but I couldn't and wasn't trying to hear anything he was saying. He was just hollering. "What the fuck is you talking about?" I finally heard him ask.

"nicca you know what I'm talking about! The same bish that was t momma funeral decided to have someone DM me acting like someone else."

He was still screaming, "Where you get that from?"

"Does it really matter who I got it from? I couldn't go through your phone. Your phone with you in prison and I'm in Atlanta--hundreds of miles away."

He must have called back about 3 million times because it felt like I answered 3 million times. I knew at that moment I still wasn't ready to leave this nicca. I felt that I needed to stay down. It could be a stupid thing to feel. The crazy part about it all was that, yeah, I felt some kind of way, but, in my mind, I was like, *'Fuck it. He in survivor mode.'* I was out there in the world in survivor mode too, however I never let him know that.

It was one thing to play me on the street but, while you in jail? Come on, at this point, you're doing the most; you're really doing too much! I still stayed down, though. I fell back a little bit, but still answered the phone when he called, still made sure he was good. I just did it on my own time. I still did things for him, but it was what I wanted to do and when I wanted to do it. He still knew he could pick up the phone call me, and I'd answer. He put me in that position, so he had to roll with the punches. A nicca is going do what he wants to do and either you're going to deal with it or move around. There is no in between. None! I had always asked him not to put me in a position as to where I had to do something to him or somebody he was dealing with because I wasn't going to let anybody play with me--keep that shit in line. Anyone that I was talking to or dealing with knew one thing: when his feet hit the concrete, it was over and you were either gone fuck with me or you weren't.

This time, I really fell back for a minute. I mean, this had happened in January and I decided in October to go visit. It had been a while and I did miss him. I didn't care how much I fell back. We were still engaged. He was still saying that I was going to be his wife and I still felt I was. The whole way there, I remembered having the bubble guts. I didn't know if I was nervous because I hadn't seen him in awhile, or if I was nervous because I thought someone else there. At this time he was in a new facility. It wasn't a big person, as it was a smaller, older jail. Everything was on paper--the sign in and everything. When I got to the front, I was asked for my identification. I gave the worker my ID and he gave me some papers out of a folder. Every inmate had their own folder of visitors. The officer pulled out some papers that held the name of all visitors from a week ago. I stood there, shaking like a leaf, thinking, *'I know this nicca didn't' have a visit last week. Oh, this definitely my last time. I will see you when you get out.'*

This nicca had lost his mind. I had been down for him for the past six years. We weren't fucking we didn't have any children together. He didn't leave me any money when he left these street. We weren't even cool when he left the streets. I was just being loyal, fucking with him tough, and he didn't even keep it real with me. I wasn't tripping about anybody jocing him because if I was in that situation, every nicca I knew was going to pop me off. It wasn't like I would have been giving any pussy away, but the difference was that I wouldn't have anyone thinking I was coming home to them, knowing I was in a relationship with someone else. I guess the saying is true: *men can't do what women do.*

As soon as he walked into the meeting area, I got up to meet him--something I never do. He had a smirk on his face, looking like, *'What's up?'*

"You want something to eat or drink?" I asked.

He said nah I'm good, but I knew him and he knew me. He could tell something was up, so he changed his mind. "Yeah, let me get a snack," he said. We were at the vending machine and I was just laughing.
"You got something you want to tell me?" I asked lightly. "No, bruh. What's up?"
I said, "I'ma ask you again...you got something you wanna tell me? Do you have anything you wanna tell me that will stop me from coming to see you again?" I watched him. He was about to say no, but he must have saw the look on my face. Before he could say anything, I told him that he had been having visits.

He admitted it and put his head down. "You know I ain't coming back, huh?" I said. "He said I know bruh."

"Well, if you aint coming back, why you don't leave now," he said.

I replied, "I drove too far. We gone ride this one out, but I ain't coming back after this." I told him that I didn't care how bad he wanted to go against what he had said. You have to lay your law down: if somebody doesn't give you your respect, you have to take it. At that moment, I knew I had to show him because, all this time, I had never disrespected him or been out in the open with anybody. He was going to respect me and after I left that day, he knew I wasn't coming back and I didn't. No matter how bad I wanted to see him, how bad I missed him, how much I needed to look in his face and talk to him, to tell him certain things that were going on, I never went back to visit.

Of course, I missed him. I missed the fuck out of him, I wanted to see him, but I wanted him to respect me and our relationship in the future more. If there was going to be a future for us, I had to lay some rules down. I told him from the start to keep it real with me. I was always upfront with him. I didn't give him details, but I let him know when I was moving around. If something did come back to him, it wouldn't have been a surprise. He could stand up and say, *'Oh yeah, D...keep it G, she told me. 'D solid. She really living like that.'* But fuck, obviously that wasn't good enough.

CHAPTER 8 - Down For Me

For the next two years, I felt so free. I felt like everything that I was holding back from I could do it and not feel bad. I was doing things I wanted to do, no matter if that meant I was going out of town, meeting new niccas, meeting new friends and not caring how he or anyone else felt. I was just living with no regrets. I got rid of the thoughts of doing my job as a girlfriend, as a fiancé, as a soon-to-be wife because, in all actuality, it wasn't reality. He was in jail and I was on the streets. He was doing whatever he had to do to make provisions for him, while I was surviving. Nevertheless I still lived life with the thought of us being together whenever he came home.

I was having fun, but I still felt like something was missing. No matter how much fun I had, how much money I made, I still felt like something essential was missing and whatever held call that spot felt filled. I didn't want to feel that way. I started to find out and search for what and who I really was. I had a few bumps in the road. I ended up opening a salon, knowing that I didn't want to do hair anymore. Besides I was good at hair. It was my gift, not my passion anymore. But I knew it was money. No matter what, when it came to doing hair, all I had to do was see a style and I could do it. The hair salon only lasted about nine months, until I closed it down and sold everything. I got back into my lipstick line. I sold all of the lipstick, which really was good for me, but again, everything I ever did was about a quick hustle. Because I was used to making and getting so much fast money quick, I didn't know what to do with it in the long run. I never took it seriously to the point where I was willing to reinvest in my business. I would spend it, not working and doing things as the millionaire in the making I want to be. I wondered how I was going to be a woman that was going to open doors for other females. What was my real journey? I couldn't just feel like me being this Down Ass Bitch was going to get it because it wasn't. I was still lacking something. It felt like the days were getting harder and harder. It felt like everyone that was close to me was just disappearing or drifting away. My best friend went to jail. TJB was still in jail. Tia left and went to Dubai. Jon started a new brand. And was picking up new clients that required him to travel 75% of the time. What the fuck was I doing?

It hit me suddenly that everyone was sacrificing something. What did I need to sacrifice? I used to just pray and cry and ask God, '*What is my sacrifice? What do I need to do?*' It turned out that my ultimate sacrifice was being alone. I needed to be alone. I needed to focus on me. I wasn't focused on a relationship. I wasn't focused on being with him. I was just living and figuring out what was best for me. I started getting into all kinds of different gigs, from the lipstick, to doing laser lipo, to helping Tia run her hair company. It was crazy because I really traveled a lot. Tia had this big photo shoot coming up for the hair company and she called me and was like, "Bitch, I see you, in and out of town. What's up? You making money or you bullshitting?"

She's like a little, big sister because she is very structured. And anyone who knows me, knows that I have no structure; my life is always all over the place. So, when she was mad or didn't think I was going to hold down my end of the bargain, she wasn't having it. When she saw me out of town or turned up, she would

call or text like, *'Oh, well, if you not going to make it, don't worry about it.'*

It always had me thinking, *'Bitch, I'm going to make it. Don't worry about the shenanigans I have going on.'* Whatever I had going on, I was going to do that. Now it's the day of the shoot. It was a Sunday. I had just flown back home from God knows where. I don't even remember where I was, but I flew back home to do this photo shoot for her. She would always tell me about this studio that she loved so much and that the people over there were so cool.

I said, laughing, "You know I don't like humans like that." "No bitch, you going to like them. They're cool." she replied.

I was still wasted from the day before. I had flew out that morning and tried to go to church. I didn't make it, so I just turned around and went straight to the photo shoot. That day I wore the same shirt Felicia had on in the movie *Friday*. It was literally the same shirt and some blue jeggings. I walked into the studio and I knew a couple of the photographers that were there from previous work, which made the setting great. My cousin, Don was there slaying per usual. I was there physically but, mentally I was somewhere else. I wasn't at the happiest place but I was doing alright. I was OK because I was moving forward with life, putting my book together and trying to stay focused. It just felt like things had started moving in slow motion.

There was this guy at the studio who kept coming in and asking if everyone was all right. I assumed that he must have been the little worker at the studio. He was dressed down. I think he had on a T-shirt and some joggers I know he had dreads. My friends always tell me to get my head out of my phone and, at the time, my head was all in my phone. I wasn't really paying that much attention to him. Yet after the third time he'd asked if I was ok, I was like, *'Damn, what do you want? We keep saying no!'*

I looked up because he said, "Hey, does anybody want anything? I'm going to make a run." Once I looked up, we made eye contact and I was like wait, "he's cute and sexy too."

I don't know if it was just a spur of the moment thing or it was just gas, but I uttered, "I do want to ask you something,

I'll wait until you come back. But can you bring me Zaxby's?"

"'Sure," he said. "I'll just get my assistant to go get it." Now, I was thinking, *'Your assistant? Oh, so you not the little worker?'* He came and sat next to me in a very business-like manner. We talked for about two hours on and off. Because he was still working. He would come back and talk to me. I told him that I was in the process of writing a book. I also told him I wanted do a short movie. He told me that we could do that, there at the studio. By time the conversation ended, we were giving each other sweet eyes (he said he wasn't). It kind of scared me because, at that time, I had about seven to eight years of being a Down Ass Bitch under my belt with TJB. And the thought of seriously dating had never crossed my mind until now. I never let myself get into that space. It was usually nothing more than some fun and some money. I mean, I never let anybody get close enough to me. I wasn't ever open to it, because I believed that TJB was going to be my husband. Yet the difference now is that we were broken up. My heart was broken. I didn't even think another man could ever get that close to me again. But I was also very vulnerable.

After the shoot was over, we exchanged numbers. Later, we literally talked the night away. We left the shoot at 12 a.m. and we talked on the phone until five that morning, like teenagers. It felt like this was the feeling that I was missing. There was somebody right there in front of my face, making me feel how I had been feeling with the person that wasn't there. My friends would always say that I lived in a fantasy world, I did I was happy in it too because I knew one day my fantasy would become reality. From that day on, we went on a date every single day. I mean every single day. It didn't matter if it was just lunch; it didn't matter if it was breakfast. It didn't matter if it was me going to the studio while he worked. As long as we were together, it felt right. I didn't know what to do, I was so happy but I still didn't have closure with TJB. I wanted these things with him.

Man, it was crazy, like really crazy. In the span of a month, we were damn near living together. But for some reason, things started to not feel right. It had me thinking, *'What's going on?*

What the fuck is going on? What are you doing?' While this was going on, TJB's release date was getting closer and closer and I was in a relationship and was happy. I never thought after all these years I'd even take someone else serious knowing me and TJB never really had closure, but that time I was very vulnerable. As I've stated previously: loyalty is everything to me. My word is everything. So I explained the situation to my new boo. I was like, *'Listen, I told my ex when he get out that I was gonna pick him up, no strings attached. I'ma go pick him up, make sure he straight. Just to get everything off our chest and let it go.'*

I don't regret it because the type of woman I am requires whoever I'm with to be as secure as possible. I know I can make a man feel insecure and I don't want anybody or anything to be able to come to you and make you feel less than or feel like I'm not who I say I am. I didn't want him to feel that I would do anything to play him. So, with things moving so fast, that was something I had to tell him for us to move forward. Yes, it brought some tension into our relationship, but I thought it gave us a stronger bond overall. What bitch was going tell their new dude that they were going to go get their ex-fiancé from jail after doing 11 years? Bitches weren't doing that and niccas damn sure weren't going to accept that.

It was about three weeks until TJB's release and things had started to change. I didn't see it at first. Out of the blue, my boo pointed out, "Ain't it almost time for you to go get your people, huh?"
I looked at him like, "*Who?*" I was in a happy place. I wasn't thinking about going get nobody from jail--at best, I would call him an Uber. I had turned over a new leaf. I responded, "That's why I told you upfront because I didn't want to have to go through this. I gave you the option to deal with me how wanted to and if you thought it would be a problem, we could have just been friends until this was out of the way. But you knew what was up."

He said, "No, you good. I'm just saying."

I really think he wasn't being honest with himself. He was still saying he wasn't tripping about me going. I knew at that moment what I was going to do. I probably shouldn't have gone, but because I was a Down Ass Bitch, I couldn't go against my word. It was the principle of the matter for me. I had infidelities and insecurities about what was going on like what if he would had come home when he said he was coming home? This man was finally coming home and I had stated to take someone else serious. I had opened a new door and never closed the old one. It took seven years, almost eight, for me to even walk out the door and be okay with it being closed. Well, I thought I was okay. I battled with that choice. I really battled everyday with the decision I was making. Considering my new relationship, something urged me not to even go pick up TJB, but I had to that was my friend before anything and my word was my word and I stood on it. This new guy was battling with me and battling with himself. I knew he didn't really want me to go, but since I told him upfront and he agreed, he knew he couldn't take it back. Honestly, it was nothing he could have said or done . I was going to get TIB. I waited almost 9 years to see him walk out of those gates. I should have made the executive decision to not even tell him. My cousin Don and my best friend Red would always say I give a nicca too much tea. We would have the most intimate conversations, talking about having a future that scared me, because in the back of my head, I knew this might not have been the right decision at the time, because I was still in love with TJB and the dreams we had over those years.

I finally had the chance to walk away from such a lengthy relationship, and try something. I'd only been dating this new dude for three months, but it was an amazing three months. I was so happy and everything I wanted was happening. I felt like this was everything I had prayed for, but remember, the enemy knows your prayer as well. I had asked God to make a change in me and it was happening right before my eyes. For me to be a better person, the woman that God called me to be, I needed a push. This guy came in the pushing and I wasn't ready to be pushed. I mean, we sat for two hours talking about my trailer for my book and a month later, the trailer was out. He made it perfect, from the strip club that he built in the middle of the studio, to paying a restaurant to shut down for filming. It was just like I was in my fantasy world, and he didn't mind being a part of it, well at the beginning. Knowing I had a 25 thousand dollar vision with a 10,000 budget, he made it happen.

Of course, I paid him. Only because this was his business and he was providing me a service. Now I didn't spend the whole budget...of course I didn't. I never wanted him to feel like I was the girl I used to be, not with him anyway. I wanted him to feel just as secure as he made me feel. But in reality he wasn't that secure and that wasn't something I could fix.

I was trying so hard to show this man that I wasn't there to hurt him or use him, I should have never let it go as far as I did. At that time in my life, I was way too vulnerable. I thought what I had was gonna make it all better and I'd somehow forget about my past. That's when my past started to haunt me. It caused me to put a guard up and act out. When things occurred, I expected him to react a certain way and he wouldn't. I was left feeling like his fight to be with me wasn't as strong as mine because I was provoking him only to receive the opposite results. However, I still wanted him to stick around because if it was me I'd stay.

That was my character not his: being a Down Ass Bitch. That wasn't the type of person he was, though. He'd rather walk away and hurt, but I always asked him, "What are you walking away from if this is what you want?" Knowing that I didn't know what I wanted. Or did I know what I wanted and it just wasn't him? I was trying to fill a void.

We all have stayed in situations longer than we should. I am the perfect person to stand here and say I have definitely stayed in a situations longer than I should have. I believe that if you want something so bad, you have to put up a good fight to get it. You'll never know the true outcome if you don't. It's much easier to walk away, but if you feel like you want something bad enough and it's worth it, you'll fight. But know this: you can't fight by yourself, love is a 2-man sport.

CHAPTER 9 - Down For the Ride

TJB's release date had finally come. I flew to New Orleans about 2p.m. I had to pick up a rental car to drive nearly four hours to the prison. It was October 25, 2018, around 11:15 p.m. I was sitting in the parking lot of the prison, nervous and anxious, waiting for him to be released. My new boo and I weren't really talking, at this time. We were still speaking to each other, but there was a lot of tension. I was still trying to do my part, trying to make him feel secure. I even texted to tell him that I was at the prison waiting and that I would call him when I was heading back. No response! So, of course, now I had a little attitude. There I was, once again tryna make him feel more secure and he was shutting me down. But whatever.

I was sitting there, waiting and thinking, *'I'ma say this, I'ma say that'*--yada yada yada. I sat there and watched the gate for Forty-five minutes until, finally, a white truck pulled up. I could see him. Like, nobody will ever understand the feeling of waiting and wanting something for so long and then *finally* seeing them face to face. Everything that I had planned to say went away. I felt like I felt eight years ago. There was a feeling of hope, a feeling of relief, bubbling up inside me. Damn, it was finally happening. I felt like a child waiting on their Christmas gifts the night before Christmas. The anxiousness I experienced in that moment was unexplainable and so different from what I'd thought I feel. His first words to me were, "Girl, get in the car. I don't wanna be nowhere around here."

We both busted out laughing and when I got in the car, we immediately pulled off. The entire ride, I just kept saying, "You're really home. You are really home." I was repeating it because we had waited for this moment for so long and now the time has come and I was in Atlanta dating, wow. I never should have been dating if we were together or not. My plan, after me and TJB broke up, was to be single for a full year to figure things in my life out. But when you make decisions based on your emotions, there's always a catch. I definitely was caught up. I didn't have to get nasty about the things that we had been through, but we did talk about that. The ride was four hours long. We talked about everything, got everything off our chests. I told him that I didn't know what the future would bring or what God had in store for us. I said, "Right now, you and I aren't on the same page and I've accepted that. But I couldn't just not come get you." I told him I thought about it, thought about saying that I wasn't coming to get him. But in the end, it was something I felt like I needed to do. I kept my word.

I picked him up, made sure he had some things he needed and I left. Yes, there was a lingering feeling of 'what if?' as I left, but I was not willing to go through the ringer with all the drama I knew would come with him after doing eleven years in prison. We both had caused each other pain due to the circumstances, but we loved each other no matter what. Loving someone doesn't always mean you're supposed to be together. I was okay with that. I really was okay with that. We decided we would be friends and be cool. Eventually, I told him I had been dating this guy for the last three months and I love how he treats me. I told him how I wanted to give it a chance that I felt it was time to do something different. But I couldn't go any further because I was still in love with him.

He told me he felt the same way. He was in New Orleans fucking off, but nothing serious because if he wasn't with me it was fuck heauxs, I want my wife. Those were his exact words. I knew what came with a man coming home from doing almost twelve years in prison. Yes, I knew he loved me. Yes, I believed he wanted me to be his wife. The real question was if I believed *he* was ready for something like that? No, he absolutely was not. Now, with him home, I was confused and didn't know exactly what I wanted. I did know that I didn't want any parts of other females or street shit. I wanted to get different results and the only way I could do that was by doing something different. I had to take a chance and I did. I went back to Atlanta the next morning. I called dreads and asked if he could pick me up from the airport. We hadn't talked for a minute, so the ride back was awkward. It was real quiet, real strange, because when we were together, everything was usually happy and fun.

That day, the atmosphere between us was dry as fuck. For me to be so open with the situation and for him to say nothing at all, puzzled me. It kind of threw me off. I tried to open up a conversation, but it pretty much died down within seconds. I had asked him if there was anything he wanted to ask me about the pickup. He swerved the conversation and dropped me off without saying anything. A couple of hours later, he decided to send a text and ask me what happened. After the lack of communication before, I decided to play stupid. I pretended that I didn't know what he was talking about, even though I knew exactly what he was getting at. He had just got out of the car with me; why did he not ask me when I was in his presence? I had the chance to look him in his eye and tell him what happened or look him in his face and lie. Whatever the case, he wasn't man enough to talk about it when he should have. So, now I had an attitude I was like, *'Why you didn't ask me when I was in your face?'* We went back and forth, in between text messages, for a

While until he was like, *'Don't worry about it. I don't want to know.'* I told him that he wanted to know from the moment I picked him up but you were scared of the truth and didn't want to feel I lied to your face so you said nothing. Now I have nothing to say.

The whole situation just did something to my new outlook and I knew that it was going to be a problem. And it truly was.

My boyfriend hadn't been coming to the house and I was giving TJB his space. It seemed like that was working for him, so I was really in my bag. I felt like something was missing, though. I didn't know if it was the fact me and TJB weren't where we had planned on being or, if it was the fact that I had decided to move on, possibly making the wrong decision. I cried every day for like a week, until one day, I decided to take action. I needed to get something off my chest. I called dreads and told him every feeling and every emotion that I was going through. He said, "Listen, I knew what I was dealing with when I met you--the good, the bad and the ugly. I saw how real it was. It was worse than I thought it was, but I love you and I'll be here and go through this with you and we gone be alright." It felt like a burden was lifted off me.

Emotionally and mentally, I was already a wreck because this was what I   wanted from TJB. When going through the transition of becoming a new person and renewing my mind from the past, I knew TJB wasn't on the same level with me mentally or spiritually. I had to fight with the fact that if I take this road, it wouldn't be easy. I knew I wasn't in position to go through the growing stage of a 38 year old man who had just did almost 12 years in jail. If that experience didn't make you grow, I damn sure couldn't make you grow either, especially while I was still fighting my own battles.

It made me angry and bitter sometimes because I knew what I wanted and what I didn't want. I was willing to give dreads a chance and finally let my past go, but he also had his own demons he was fighting. I started praying even harder. I know how the enemy works. I knew he was coming at any moment. He was going to try and use all his old tricks to set you back and if I wasn't ready to go to war, I'd fail. I knew he was trying and using his best shit, but I was at a place where I could see past that. I kept fighting for me and I started focusing on myself. The devil hadn't been able to break me like he used to.

Now I hadn't talked to TJB in about three weeks. I felt like we cleared the air and was in a good space. I didn't want to smother him, especially after telling him I was dating and taking it seriously. I said, "Fuck that. I'm calling his stupid ass." I was out there in Atlanta, going through the motions because all I could really think about was the life we had planned. Now he was out of jail and we weren't together. What the fuck was going on? Was he in NOLA, living his best life? No sir, not without me. I called and, of course, he answered. I tried my best to be as calm as possible, but that didn't happen. I went all in, only for him to say that this was what I had wanted. He said he had wanted his family, but I was the one who left him behind in the trenches. It's just like a nicca to make you feel like shit when you already feel bad. He wasn't really acknowledging the facts, that he didn't even try to put up a fight, by the end of the conversation, we were ok. Everything was alright at the moment. The holidays were rolling around and I was bored and lonely. I decided to do what was once normal for me. I started going out again, trying to be back on the scene. I was feeling dumb as fuck, though. It wasn't what I wanted to do. It wasn't the new me. I'd rather be at home, getting ready for thanksgiving, cooking, shopping and doing family shit. On Thanksgiving day, at 12 a.m., I got a text from him, *Happy Thanksgiving.* Before I looked at the name, I knew it was him. It felt just like when he was in jail, wanting to be the first at everything. I was happy to see the text, thinking, *'Ah, I know you feeling how I'm feeling. We should be together.'* But right after those happy feelings, my instincts kicked in. He must have been with a bitch because why else was he texting me at that time of morning? I texted back and said, *'Why you text me? Call me.'* The iPhone bubbles started to pop up and I was pissed. I knew what was up and I started with the shits: I facetimed him--no answer. I called him--no answer. He kept texting as I cursed him out and blocked him. I was standing in the kitchen, cooking and feeling played all at the same time.

I tried to start a new relationship knowing I wasn't healed from my past. I was still in a confused state. I still felt like something was missing. I was fighting with my flesh and what I wanted versus what I know I needed to do. For the past eight and half, almost nine years, I had been a DAB living in a fairytale. I was living and operating with the thought that when TJB came home, all my dreams would come true. My friends would always say that I lived in a fairytale world and I finally realized I really was. Day in and day out, week after week, month after month, year after year, I believed that once we were together, everything would just happen like magic.

It's funny how people would act as though they don't understand the same situation, or can relate; we're all Down Ass Bitches in some way shape, form or fashion. As women we get with men and they become our priority. The relationship itself becomes our priority because we all long to be a wife and have a family.

We're willing to put ourselves aside to make things work, to make things right, to make it fit. You can't force it, though. Once that title is there, we just subconsciously move in that aspect.

God made us to be nurturers, so we nurture

the situation, not realizing we are putting fertilizer on who we are and our goals. Then, we look back and realize we put ourselves to the side to build someone else up. Now, you have to restart who and what you want to do and be. It's not impossible to do both, but you have to be mentally prepared to do such, as well as your partner. That's why the bible says we must be equally yoked, meaning: both individuals must be on the same page in what and where they want to go in life. Both must be willing to make the necessary sacrifices to get there.

Everyone will not be ready and willing at the same time. You have to make the choice to either stick with that person until they get there, which will come with a lot of test, trials and tribulations--constantly asking yourself: *Is this person worth it?*--or, move forward and continue to build yourself into the person you want to be. If it's meant to be, that person will level up or God will remove them from your path but, you have to be willing to remove yourself from the situation.

After talking to TJB on the regular, we decided we would give us a try. We were going to be together again and start putting our goals and plans to work. Letting go of our past and moving forward on to the things we dreamed about. I was going to move back to New Orleans for six months to a year and we'd stay there, stack money and move back to Atlanta once we got our businesses in order. I made an investment of $500 into a new business, all while I was a month behind on releasing this book. I had writers block. I was so wrapped up and confused about what was going on that I couldn't focus on me. On the other hand, the new business took off fast in New Orleans. I was there more than I was in Atlanta, so, of course, now it was easier for me to cling to TJB and he was just as clingy to me. He wanted to pull up, talk, and go on dates, all while still playing and doing slick shit that I had no idea he was doing. I was trying to keep my composure and stay in the dating zone, but with our history that didn't work on either end because we both felt we held the same position in each others' lives. We both felt like we had seniority and we did. If I said stop, he stopped. If he said jump, I said, '*How high?*' However, that still wasn't enough to repair the damaged we'd caused. The difference was that I was willing to move forward and work on building what we once had back with no strings attached. It would just be me and him, but his vision was different.

He looked at the situation as sort-of trade off: while he was gone, I had been living, so now, it was his time to live. He'd say he wasn't holding the boyfriend thing over my head, but he was.

His actions showed me he was a real nicca, per say, which, I wasn't interested in. I was waiting for and wanting the man I fell in love with almost nine years ago. He wasn't able to express his hurt and get through it one day at a time and build what he really wanted. Every day, he would say, "Man I just "But, what?" I would ask, but I already knew. I knew I couldn't make him be a man. He had to grow and make that decision on his own. Day after day, I tried. I did everything in my power to still be a Down Ass Bitch. I was willing to stay and go through whatever came with being with him because I know what we once shared was great. I knew he loved me. I knew he wanted to be with me and have a family, I also knew he wasn't truly ready for any of that. That was the scariest part of it all.

My business was booming and he had a good job. I managed to see past what was in front of us. I saw all the things we talked about, those long nights on the phone, those visits to the prison, those moments we shared daydreaming about when he'd come home, how we were going to work hard for a year, grind and then start a family. It was all right there, but it wasn't happening like that. It felt like my dream had turned into a nightmare. I go through these emotional ups and downs, fighting with myself and blaming myself for things he would do and say. I dealt with having to face my friends and family saying I was stupid (which, I didn't really care about). I was seeing him with other females. At times, I felt like, *'Fuck it. He just came home. He gotta get that out his system.'* But I was also realizing that I didn't have to stick around until he got anything out of his system. I had been down long enough and if he couldn't see that after all this time, it was his lost, not mine.

The crazy thing was that I still wasn't completely done with him. I still wanted the fairytale to turn into reality. So, I continued to stay down and things were actually working out ok. It seemed like life was getting better. Little things would happen, but I'd brush it off because it was nothing major. Christmas was rolling around, things were going good and we were in a good space. It was our first Christmas together after nine years and his first Christmas home with his family after almost twelve years. Everyone was happy. We cooked on Christmas Eve and went to everyone's house Christmas Day. New Years came around and it was like magic. A new year implied a new me and a new start. I was with the love of my life standing downtown by the RiverWalk on New Year's Eve watching the ball drop. We weren't on the phone, pressing one, saying '*Happy New Year*', but face to face. Tears rolled down my face and I was as happy as ever. He looked into my eyes and told me that he was here now, told me not to cry. I couldn't believe he was really home. I was so filled with happiness and peace. I was ready to move forward and leave everything from the past in the past. When it came to me and TJB, nothing else mattered.

About a week later, I went back to Atlanta. I needed to get things in order with the apartment and figure out my next move. Was I gonna stay in Atlanta or move home to work on us? Again, business was booming in New Orleans. I decided again that this was what I wanted. My heart wanted it so bad, plus he wanted the same thing. All there was left was to try and make it work.

While I was out there, things had seemed a

little off. I do admit that we did get into it before I left, but that was normal for us. We fussed and fought all the time, but this time, it felt different. After being with someone so long, you get to know them and, I mean, we knew each other well. So, I was still staying positive like, *'You made the decision to keep on being down bish, don't trip.'* The problem was that he didn't seem as happy as he was before I left. It was like he wasn't excited, like he wasn't himself.

came back maybe four days later. He picked me up from the airport and I was so happy to see him. I got in the car and he looked stressed. I asked him what was wrong as I eyed the sweat popping off his forehead. He was hollering out shit like, *'Liiiiiiffffeee.'*

I was thinking, *'I know this nicca not on drugs. Do he have Tourette syndrome or something?'* Something was definitely wrong. "Boy, what the fuck is wrong with you? Talk to me." He told me that he was going to talk to me later, after I got off work. Consequently, all day at the shop, I kept trying to think of what he could possibly have to tell me. I did like one client and rescheduled the rest of my clients. I called him about an hour later to come pick me up. I got in the car and there it was: the syndrome started kicking in again. I said, "Boy, look, come on say what you have to say." Silence greeted me. Then, he suddenly looked at me. I could see the fear in his eyes, so I put my head down and looked at my phone to try and distract how I started to feel. I knew that this was something serious.

He said, "Man, she said she," he paused and took a deep breath, "PREGNANT!" Immediately, when he said *'she said'*, I knew what was going to come after that. I blacked out. My stomach sunk to the floor. I literally couldn't even talk. He kept saying, "Say something please, D. Say something." I couldn't utter a word. Nothing would come out. I was numb. It felt like was paralyzed, I literally couldn't move or say anything.

was broken all over again, but this time it felt like shattered glass. So much was running through my head. I didn't know if I was coming or going. I just knew I had to get away from him before I hurt him. I texted Diva and said, *'Code red. Please meet me at your house now.'* I told him that I had to get out of this car and to drop me off at Diva's. Now he was talking, but I didn't know what he was saying. I literally couldn't hear anything, I was in a daze. I still don't know what he said.

Diva pulled up, I got in the car and fell in her arms like a baby. "What's wrong?" she asked, as I was shaking. "What the fuck did he do? What happened?"

I told her what happened and she looked at me with the most hurtful look, hugging me tight. I cried like a newborn baby every day for about a week. I still had to see him every day because we had one car and we were still living together. Then, one day, I just snapped. We were in the car and I lost it. I mean, I went nuts. I fought him like I was fighting for my life. It was for my life. I felt like I wasted years waiting on him to build a family with me and marry me. He was now telling me a bitch was pregnant. Mind you, it was the same troll bitch that I told him would do anything to destroy us and he let it happen. He could have been fucking any bitch in the world and I wouldn't have cared. But I asked him not to fuck with her because her motive was to get the ups on me, which in reality was a stupid move on both their parts. He had only been home four months; he had no money saved up no car, no house, but a baby on the way. *Wow!*

No, we weren't technically together when it happened, but we were working on us. Fuck, it was too much and he was crazy enough to want me to stay, to go through this with him. But guess what? I was even crazier because I STAYED... I guess that's what good dick and love do to you. I was hurt yes, but I'd still have happy moments but no matter what Id piss myself off. I'd never let myself get too happy because I was scared to be let down again. I was praying for God to just show me and give me the strength to do whatever it is next, and He did just that.

About three months later, after still trying to work on us, fighting for what we both wanted, BOOM! Here comes another female that's pregnant with his child. YES! Another one and *he* didn't tell me. An old friend saw us tighter and said, "girl I didn't know you were still together." I said, "not really" and she replied "how you deal with two babies on the way?" Crickets.

She continued onto say who the other female was and all the other details.

I didn't tell him anything about it at first, but the next day he called me to meet him and I couldn't hold it in any longer. I met him and went the fuck off! He said after telling me about the first baby, it was no way he could have told me about the second baby so soon. He said that he didn't know for sure if they were his. I said "listen, you would say anything to keep me here. But this is it, I'm staying away from you."

I decided that I didn't have to put up with his bullshit and I still didn't mean it. I still wanted that fairytale...and that's all it was, a fairytale.

About The Author

D'Wayna Reniece Irvin

Growing up in New Orleans Louisiana, D'Wayna "Supa D" Irvin always knew that she wanted to live life on a large scale. At the age of 16, Supa D had a passion to pursue the entertainment industry. Her mocha chocolate skin and body measurements of 36DD-28-44 has caught the attention of artists and magazines across the nation. With her natural ability to camouflage compared with her modeling capabilities, Supa has always had the confidence to live her dream.

For more than four years, the Louisiana native has navigated her way through the south, showing everyone that she is here to take the industry by storm. From hosting Floyd Mayweather's appearance at Club Metropolitan in New Orleans and making special guest appearances throughout Atlanta, Texas, and Florida she does everything SUPA. Her admiration for the night life and flashing lights has provided her with the opportunity to appear in videos with hip hop

rtists such as, "Young Greatness "
"QuentOnMyGrind" and many more. She has
also served as a representative for
NoRaceNoGender clothing line, Pretty Posh
Dubai virgin hair and Haus of Saint Braitian
Lashes. Her bodacious curves and slim waist have
also appeared in "Fyne Girls Magazine, Stunnaz
Magazine, BlaCkMen, Pressure Magazine, and
Well Konnected Magazine.

A licensed cosmetologist who started a laser lipo company
"I'm fine in real life" along with her "Supa Slim Detox
Tea." Supa D also has a liquid matte stay on lipstick
collection. All while writing a book and studying
psychology.

She lives by the motto, "I always win."

Contact Information

Email:

readDABnow@gmail.com

Instagram:

iama_DAB

Facebook:

D'Wayna Irvin

Website:

readDAB.com

Mailing Address:

PO Box 93095

Atlanta GA 30377

Made in the USA
San Bernardino, CA
18 February 2020

64650315R00075